DONEGAL
SUITE

Other books by John P. McNamee

Diary of a City Priest
Clay Vessels and Other Poems
Endurance: The Rhythm of Faith

DONEGAL SUITE

by
John P. McNamee

To Rosemarey —
love John —

Dufour Editions

First published in the United States of America, 2006
by Dufour Editions Inc., Chester Springs, Pennsylvania 19425

ISBN 0-8023-1343-4 Paperback (978-0-8023-1343-0)
ISBN 0-8023-1344-2 Hardcover (978-0-8023-1344-7)
ISBN 0-8023-1345-0 LSE (978-0-8023-1345-4)

Cover Art: *Gweedore* (Bog Series) by Anne Stahl
Author photo taken by Eugene Martin

Library of Congress Cataloging-in-Publication Data

McNamee, John P., 1933-
  Donegal suite / by John P. McNamee.
    p. cm.
  ISBN 0-8023-1344-2 (hardcover)
  ISBN 0-8023-1343-4 (pbk.)
  ISBN 0-8023-1345-0 (limited signed hardcover)
    1. Donegal (Ireland) -- Poetry. 2. Christian poetry, American.
  I. Title.

PS3563.C388364D66 2006
811'.54--dc22
                                        2006016843

Printed and bound in the United States of America

Table of Contents

FOREWORD

This deeply nourishing book is set in two countries, two continents, but also voyages into inner and outer mystery — the great ocean, as well as the cloud, of unknowing. The physical settings and their cultures are particular: Donegal, a rural region of protean beauty in northwest Ireland, and bleak urban neighbourhoods of North America. Seemingly disparate worlds and their communities share consonance and dissonance, and both yield their epiphanies to the receptively-tuned sensibility of John McNamee. The human and historical bonds between those worlds are the deep links of Ireland and America that plumb far beyond the facile or sentimental into an archaeology of countless lives and destinies.

Our oldest and most transcending tradition of all, however, is the common fact that we are human, and this condition inescapably involves us in the mystery of being. The truly rewarding grace of *Donegal Suite* is that while it draws on a learned and profound wealth of spiritual awareness, faith and tradition, it is also humble in its struggle, its wonderment and its insights, divining springs and trickles of revelation, hope and love in the earthiness of what's specific, broken and everyday. In the course of "this vigil which is always inconclusive" there is also story, light and shadow and transfiguration, as well as wit and warmth for savour and for blessing — as there should be in all that's human and incarnate.

Poetry is an especially organic art and human instinct. It grows in its own time, out of the lived life. It can't be planned. It can't be faked. The poems here are earned in living out the singular days and nights and all their sung or unsung instances. As he encounters the individual humanity and dignity of poor people on an inner city bus and the meeting sheds unbidden light upon him, the author is lifted into love: *this bus would be a good place to die.*

It's all there, and finally a song of joy.

— Michael Coady

I

Homecoming

Earth and sea and air might mean nothing more
than elements around us, a stage where our self -
contained bodies move and maneuver.

What I know is that one wild afternoon on
the Giant's Causeway in County Antrim
wind and salt-spray, the smell of kelp and a
walk on wet lichen-covered basalt columns
was home as never elsewhere am I home.

My long-dead father's place not fifty
kilometers south. He, Scots and Irish, and
if sight could pierce the horizontal rain, there
the Mull of Kintyre north across the water.

Tousled and wet, I returned to an inn
back from the headland where the smell
of tobacco on damp wool mixed with
the odors brought from their farms by
old men gathered with pints around a fireplace.
A home I was visiting for the first time.

Hedgerows

The disappointment that the fuchsia
are so overgrown. All year I have been
eager for this borrowed house.
The sea in distant view a reason why
this place and not some other.

Now it is like any other unless
I rise from my chair and stretch into
the wind that shakes the pendulous
blossoms   this summer morning of
laundry blowing on lines hooked
to houses as small across the fields as
the sheep out day and night in this season.

Come back to the closeby.   Without
bruising them take in hand like bunches
of grapes the lantern-like fuchsia as
wondrous in shape and color as the sea
which after all is worth the stretch.

Donegal Morning

Morning reveals what night had whispered
a rain trying to own the day as well.
Hope can be small: I imagine some
Awareness up there that with daylight

I want to be out and about without an umbrella
pulling me into the wind   without the splash from
a passing car on a shoulderless road.
I expect some consideration from Providence.

Room to room   window to window of an empty house
I await a late clearing that will allow my return to the
headland where the sun falling into the sea takes me
beyond my impatience for better weather.

Weather

The forecast was rain   yet
here at noon the day is holding.
From the sea clouds mount in
long horizontal billows in the
pattern of the blanket around me.

Uneasy with the quiet
I wander between chores and books
room to room. Is that sunlight
out the window? No. Just different shading.

Finally I note that dark
day and sky mirror me   my
shapeless worry wants relief.

With umbrella as a walking stick
I will stride the half-hour to the church.
Walking and sitting   I will accept this
mood as a place from which to pierce the clouds.

Gweedore Chapel

The Church is over-sized   as hard
inside as out. A granite tone to
match the surrounding fieldstone.
Even the green carpet everywhere
seems meant to fade into the gray.

Hard to pray here. We can
find our hearts hard. The trouble
is the altar end   yet any sense of a stone
ear there is false. We are heard.

Odd how these accidents are important.
God is in the details is a consequence
of the Incarnation. Everything is human.
The importance of architecture.

Seminary Summers At Home

Fifty years later I remember the weeks:
up before six   opening the dark church
tending the Masses before a day painting and
cleaning in impossible heat in an empty school

until the five o'clock return to the church
setting up for the next morning   then
disappearing into the darkness until
the Angelus. I can still feel the coarse
rope   the long walk home to dinner.

Those years give me no expectations
of this hermitage   no deliverance
from the lifelong Cloud of Unknowing
which says that the mystery is unavailable
to our understanding   only to the will
by love

I attend.   I fall away.   I redirect
as gently (the instruction) as a feather on a pillow.
The return is the loving.   The empty space
a human place if only that I am there.

Diversion

In the remove the appetites appear
even my few morning prayers are rushed
clock-watching for a first coffee.

A walk into the village for necessities
becomes the sight of a woman in summer dress
unaware of my eyes in the shop

where a news stall is all pictures
and words of little consequence
inviting a curiosity   which in
the monastic tradition is a vice.

Regimen

"No phone   no radio or music"
the advice of an old monk versed in these spaces.
Music is already a lack.   For years
I try to inhabit the silent spaces between notes
since the rest of life is sound.

We are made to connect.
The awareness that no one will be arriving
makes even a mechanical sound a comfort:
the clothes washer filling and emptying
cars passing by   reassurance of a world
I thought more easily left behind.

The demon is doubt
the silence like nothingness.
The comings and goings I escape are
at least real   resist touch   welcome kindness

Yet the spaces are as necessary as the notes.
I shall stay here to be better there.

Habitare Secum

Away from the familiar
the aim is emptiness except for
an occasional glance at the calming sea.

Books   pencil   blank pages   are
relief from the vacant spaces within
that both invite and frighten.

I weaken. The evening hour after
a solitary meal is hard   worsened
by lights in the homes among the hills.

I succumb. A cabinet in the next room
has spirits to soften the lump of self
a switch and a blank screen fills
with distracting color.

"Poetry" the listings read:
"Philip Larkin: Life and Death In Hull".
Well, I am interested in Larkin is my excuse
the screen full is darker than empty.

"Boredom and fear and with the years
more fear than boredom." And more spirits to ease
the terror and death spirits softened and hastened.

No Larkin, I return from smaller terrors
wanting to catch what Larkin missed
the Love promised *greater than our hearts.*

Evenings

Here   in summer the light lasts
until eleven   allowing a day of rain
the surprise of a late sun   bright enough
to bring me to a rise behind the house.

The expanse of sun on water such
that   sea   headland   sun   are one
luminous moving element   a glory we
should allow in us who are also mirrors.

Climate

Weather might be everything.
In Italy with summer all life is
outdoors   tourists detour
around restaurants owning the sidewalks.

Here no sidewalks at all and
walking a road without a shoulder
I choose for safety the side of oncoming cars.

Even now in August smoke and the smell of
turf drifts from cottages snug in hills
wearing brown grasses that
in the Amalfi would be only weeds.

Yet here in the bog a purple and golden carpet
thin and close from grazing sheep
an alpine meadow

"It is our tradition" someone says
"our affection for the understatement"
a small Church of Ireland chapel
almost hidden in a stand of trees

rather than the embrace of Piazza San Pietro,
say, so open that even the life of the immense
Basilica pours outdoors.

Graveyard Mass In Donegal

A traffic jam   worthy of New York
Everybody out this Sunday afternoon
to the parish cemetery   so close to
the ocean you hope the tide is out.

I can't know where they get
the black granite for the thin
upright markers   in Irish or English
telling in gold-leaf inscription:
Name   spouse or parents   place
of origin as exact as the townland.

Thousands come yearly   from as far
as Scotland . Each family at the foot
of their plot facing the gravestone
telling part of their family story.
The children behave with some
sense of the serious occasion

which is not some polite remembering
no, a prayer really   a forthright faith
in the Communion of Saints which says
faith, hope and love are stronger than death.

One ebony gravestone reads in gold:
Alana Marie Boyle died 1 April 1986 at 9 ½ months
and below that a New Testament verse:
Jesus called a little child   of course

I do not understand the Mass   all
in Irish with priests and musicians
up on the stage of the open side
of a tractor trailer   a cover for the
Ulster weather changing as you watch it.

I can read the Catholic signs:
priests going among us sprinkling graves
genuflections   the rhythm of the Our Father
the exchange of peace   Holy Communion.
The first Sunday Reading was appropriate:
the ingathering of sheep in Jeremiah.

The rain started three times   before
the sun returned. While leaving people
pointed to the rain back in the hills all
the while and explained that the laughter
at the end was the parish priest saying
how every year he prays to an old woman
buried there to keep them dry.

Teac Jack

After the Cemetery Mass   the custom
of a Sunday dinner out.   They have us
in a rear room without tablecloths for
families with small children.

Beside us a mother is off fetching
a wain wandering into the bar
her husband feeds the baby beside
him in the pram.   All the while

the newspapers shout the war which
my own country is beginning
in the Middle East.   Some relief
my brief sharing the innocence of
this small country I claim.

Tomorrow the young father will be
out early to the job providing this
pleasant afternoon   wife as well off
to work   children with her mother.

Everything has to change   how build
a home even here where Europe ends
while the world burns? Somehow
it will all reach here.

Even this lovely setting is expression of
the problem told in the film *Garden
of the Finzi-Continis* when a gentle
Italian detective in Nazi-shadowed
Italy arrives to arrest a Jewish couple

twisting his hat in two hands   anguished
by his task: "I am sorry, but I have a family."
The old Jewish gentleman turns to his wife:
"That's the trouble with Italy these days
everybody has a family."

Errigal Heritage Center

"We'll fetch you at ten. A football affair.
You'll come. We won't stay long."
Four hours later the young athletes are
easy about the time and consequences
of their many pints for Monday morning
when most are off to work somewhere.

In the bar of an inn out in the bog
their lives pint in hand are shaped more
by conversation than a Monday morning
rising or even football unless
the talk in Irish is football.

A gay Irishman, they say with no offense,
is one who foregoes football for the girlfriends,
who are along for the evening but content
for now to be off at tables by themselves.

The women have their own interests   more
dressed-up than these fellows for such is
the work of women: clothes, hair… I wonder
how these open shoes fare on the cinders.

The men are more a mystery   indifferent
to what drives their kind as close as Dublin.
Even the football more craic than machismo
and their old cars just able for work and back.

So generous with their few euros   my pint not
empty before another arrives   my benefactor
nods from the bar where with courtesy Irish
cedes to English when I approach.

L'enracinement. Simone Weil's awe of roots
in saving a language they save so much.

Leo's Pub

Though famous, the place is rural
hard to find on a Saturday night
when many will find it for the
late hour when the *craic* starts.

We were seven. Our first look
said standing room only...unless
that empty table in the middle with

the old man there...Is he alone?
His nod and wink said welcome.
Up to us to find some stools.

Gradually our sense that more
than others we had read him right.
We were welcome in a space where

every night he sits soft drink in hand
(I knew from the color and shape of his glass)
to pass the short or long Irish nights hearing
songs he has heard a thousand times.

I looked for his wedding band and saw none.
"A bachelor," I said to no one but myself,
"he comes for sound and human company.
Lovely how they let him sip one drink all night."

It was time for us to order another round and
proper to include him as he included us.
"Cola," he said above the music. I thought:
        graceful of him: ask nothing, refuse nothing.

Bloody Foreland

The beauty is the unevenness of everything.
The huge granite boulders look human -
hewn   yet not quite   as though they
tumbled down this steep sweep of land
yesterday   and their precarious lean
will have them farther down tomorrow.

Even this rock become my seat
though adequate is an uncomfortable fit
with an uneven sod carpet underneath.

The small beach far below would be
more accessible without the stone
and gravel impossible for bare feet.
Unless the beach exists just to bring
the sound of breakers flowing through
pebbles these thousands of meters up
for my hearing.

The several islands are too large
or low or close to shore. Can one
reach them at all … have they any
purpose other than nests for the sea
birds which are curiously absent?

Prayer Walk

The Exercises of Saint Ignatius say
the Mystery will be as intrusive in us
as we by listening allow. Thus

this seaside walk of hearing water
crest and fall   looking out to where
vision fails   feeling wet sand underfoot.

The cultivation of the senses. Yet
even here   distraction. We are
more the sandpipers skittish

about staying dry than fat gulls
sitting Buddha-like gazing out
            with an attention that evades me.

Bloody Foreland II

A worn picnic table with attached benches
becomes my prie-dieu. Ah, no, only
a seat to keep me here an hour or more.

Tourists stop to take in the panorama
and seeing me alone remark on the weather
assure me that the view of two promontories

embracing the sea is worth my vigil and
the silence that invites their comment.
I have no clear idea what I am about.

Occasionally an image from Francis deSales
surfaces: *Let yourself be seen*   no shadows
                    here to hide me from Heaven's eye.

Celibacy

In the color of dawn before the sun
two doves appear as usual on
the telephone wire outside my window.

They mate for life and are either a distraction
from my vigil or part of it.
One arrives before the other
the first flies off   the partner follows

as though we are at once ourselves
and whoever others make us.

An overcast keeps the morning gray
by chance or choice some of us need
an identity beyond these clouds.

Thus this vigil which is always inconclusive.

Maghereroarty

Urban renewal or such Donegal style
a new concrete causeway ending in
moorings for a small fishing fleet
a slip for the ferry that rides the
swells twice daily to Tory Island.

The descent   high road to beach
to pier so steep that we seem to be
running out onto the water where
a father and son are quiet together
wrapped in a fishing line.   Or welcoming
conversation if that's our offer.

The father, it turns out, commutes four hours
to his native Dublin every week for work.
No easy drive   Donegal people seldom
buy a used car in their own county.

Besides our words the only sounds are
the incoming tide slapping the boats
metal and rope lines lashing the masts
the smells are the floating red kelp and
the bag of mussels   our fishermen's bait

more than enough to have father hurry home
weekends to his Gaeltacht wife who speaks
only Irish to the children in his absence.
As for the mussels   the fishing was poor
the offer to us to take them home for dinner!

Belfast Dinner

Protestant or Catholic? The sad
unspoken question in Antrim even
for this nervous try at a restaurant
in an old charthouse by the quay.

From our table near the entrance
I was suddenly Dives as Lazarus
appeared framed in the glass door
not in rags just rumpled and lean
holding an empty plastic bag.

The owner saw him. Let him linger
connect with me across linen folded
into stem glasses. His nod and gesture
to his empty bag enough

to invoke the Parable summon my
few quid across the divide. On leaving
I thanked the owner for allowing him.
A kindness more generous than my own.

Dublin Area Rapid Transit

Over headlines heavy with wars
famine   floods   local crimes
I see a young mother lean into

the handle of her baby carriage for
the rise   platform to commuter train.
One task of a big job that is hers

night and day. She doesn't think
about what kind of world awaits
her charge.

Everything about her tells a
confidence that she will raise
a child ready for any world.

Wedding

Despite my street map   lost
walking Dublin on a Saturday afternoon
with no destination other than the bookshops.

Twice around Saint Stephen's Green
before the rain hurried me into University
Church.   Ah, no

I would have visited anyhow.
The necessary nod to Newman and Hopkins.
Even a young Joyce probably prayed here.

A waiting limousine and chauffeur were
notice to expect a wedding   and for me
an opportunity for Mass missed earlier

and the muffled hope I always bring to church
to lift my damp spirit into the high ceilings
along with the flame of votive lights was

for once not disappointed. The music
the flowers   the bright clothes   the joy of
wedding guests reached me seated far back

unnoticed   I stayed the while noting at length
a plaster Saint Thérèse on a pedestal nearby.
Innocent and aware she was off to

other nuptials that consumed her.
On leaving I touched her foot
asked the grace for our common cause.

Dublin Commuter

Alone. He knows by tap and count
the steps   the stops of this train.

Once inside he is still alone   standing
arm around pole his cane lowered.

His dress and manner say normalcy or
more. Success. An office and a secretary.

No hint of feeding on his hurt.
His self-possession stirs my interest:

How alone is he? Who chooses that
jacket, matches the tie, selects the shoes?

Perhaps he prays   goes to church
sees his infirmity as a parable

a grace that has him make his
way by faith. With his station

his arm extends   cane in hand.
I see a wedding band.

I am glad he goes home to her.

II

On Seeing the McGovern Print of
Annie Moore Arriving on Ellis Island

No lighter-than-air moonwalk
this landing
no
her moorings are heavier than her luggage:
indenture   child labor   coal mines
other people's laundry

At length marriage   yet even there
a life shaped by necessity
as confining as her
Father Son and Holy Ghost house

No space   no help
just the parish school where
day hours the children are away

Or the papier-mâché Lourdes shrine of
the nearby church where with Bernadette
she lifts her eyes to the Lady.

Morning Light

Brick walls dust sidewalks
with rust crumble as far
as the empty factory
worn as the body

I force snail-like
to my morning window
where sunrise now burns
glass shards and paint peel.

Downstairs a summer door
catches fire   a thousand
suns in screen door squares
the dust residue of summer.

Downtown the day still clear
later the sun on the far side
will dance   river to rose
museum columns

a shimmer warm as any hearth
lit against this October night
that blaze in us
deeper than decay.

Vigil

Empty yourself...
and sit waiting
content with the grace of God
says Saint Romuald from a card
leaning on a windowsill where
I am waiting for morning now
arriving with an orange line
the length of the horizon.

Back behind that rim the sun
is already shaping the black roof
of night into a blue dome that
promises a cloudless day. Down
east wisps linger   air brushes
a Chinese script signature   a finger-
print of the singular that is every dawn.

The frozen fingers of a naked tree
reach up   mute as my waiting
the only grace in sight: the orange
edge   blue dome growing   cloud wisps
the beauty of the world.

Images

Last winter after Christmas   a grace
leading deeper into the Incarnation
an exhibition of photographs:
Sabastião Salgado: Migrations
Humanity in Transition.

The world of the Flight into Egypt:
stable and manger leading to a road going nowhere
only each other and the clothes on their backs
their only comfort the necessary rests which
may or may not mean food and sleep.

A story still with us:
seasonal workers bent in the fields
either side the expressways ending
at restaurants where crisp salads cost
more than the day's wage made picking them.

With summer and retreat I met *Leoncio*
an *indocumentado* who walked   Guatamala
to New York and was glad for his en route
arrest   hoping he would be fed.

This parish retreat house his oasis.
Between cleaning chores he is in chapel
haunched on his heels motionless in prayer.

Africans…Mexicans…Haitians
Christ's incarnation after Christmas.
More! Arrest   imprisonment   execution.
At length bending lower than the crèche
to be with us   to be with them.

Looking Up

Across the room a fireplace
as cold as this January day
in those empty weeks when
we descend deeper into winter

at first a yearning for Spring
longer light   mild air   yet
something can be said for winter:

the quiet of empty streets
coming in from the cold
the pleasure of a sweater

with a match to kindling
that hearth can fill the room with
a glow   a warmth   worth any summer.

Horarium

I have a morning routine to help me survive the day
rather than a more modern digital timepiece
my vade mecum is the traditional wristwatch
a mirror in miniature of Dante's orbital universe:
the Love that moves the sun and the other stars

moving me downstairs to a windowless kitchen
that would frame my day in interruptions
unless I reach for the big coffee mug
black as a Benedictine cowl
handslice thick brown bread   the fare of monks
repetition as rhythm rather than tedium.

Denouement

The empty shelves unmask me
as much as a morning mirror
before a splash of water sets
my face against the day

For years the books were an accumulated identity
and more recently a false self:
lost loves   outgrown pieties
and kind gifts   more the choice of the giver

Now neither the time nor interest
to sort through them.   They all go
together with the discs and cassettes
the chant of monks that nourished me
the manna of many Lenten deserts
the milk and honey of Christmas and Easter

All boxed and taped   off to an empty space
with no real plan for recovery   here and there
a holdout   a few volumes on the nightstand
travelers' maps   a desperate hope at location

But overall a letting go   comforted by remembering
a visit to Greek ruins   a guide pointing to a stark row
of roofless columns   his gesture a revelation!

The parabolic curves of the fluted shafts
between capitals and base shaped in cypress green
and blue Agean sky amphoras suddenly visible
as real as lovely as the stones that shaped them

City Bus

On boarding I admire the courtesy of
this working woman who cradles
the huge steering wheel as ably as
she does grandchildren off somewhere in daycare

while she is in and out of traffic
stopping   starting   waiting for
old people cautious about the high step
sidewalk to bus   younger women

infants in tow searching handbags
for transit passes   she is especially patient at
this stop when she follows me to the back of the bus
where with switches and levers and seat-

belts she transforms the rear door into
a lift for a battery-driven wheelchair
and anchors in chair and passenger whom
I hardly noticed waiting with me on the sidewalk.

With a vacant stare I read the back pages of
the newspapers of the working poor   wonder
what music on his headset moves the young
guy in work shoes beside me.

It pleases me to be here. I think of Pascal
out and about in a fancy coach in Paris
seeing the poor slogging the muddy streets
inventing mass transportation.

Dying at his sister's mansion and told
he was not ill enough for Viaticum he
asked to be removed to the poor house.
If he could not expire with Christ in his heart
then he would die in Christ's.

This bus would be a good place to die.

Letting Go

Holy Week first happened outside the Temple
ended beyond the city walls.   Yet
the fewer and fewer of us still spend
most of Holy Week in church:

Palm branches   pitcher and basin   cross-raising
as though the rituals bring about what they signify.

This Easter I remember winter
a regular at the door   his familiar story:
hungry   cold   needing medicine   carfare
for the shelter of a faraway friend.

And I remember my weariness of him ...

His thin windbreaker sent me upstairs to
my sea of sweaters   scarves   gloves
even an unworn winter coat or two

And in a drawer a cashmere watch cap
apparently too precious to wear or give away.

The effort required to part with a hat ...

No easy grace   no passing over
without the back and forth
the struggle of spring over winter.

Peter and Paul

Not the Apostles   no
a couple of guys who a decade apart
landed here free fall
after half their lives locked up.

Both have that prison stride
explained to me as a macho thing:
elbows out   arms swinging
"my personal space   don't trespass."

From what I know of jail life
both are something of a miracle
like the Elizabethan vicar asked
how he managed the back and forth:
Protestant   Catholic   Protestant again
replied: "Sir, I survived!"

These two survived and more
found the faith which finds them here
learned to handle hard times
hard places like "the hole"   took

that harsh regime as Pascal's challenge:
All our troubles come from being unable
to be alone and quiet in a dark room.

The long remove leaves wounds
wary of friendship   self-directed
to a fault   yet withal a patience
with themselves as well as us.

They are accustomed to waiting.

Philip Berrigan

In a room full of friends   standing
talking   waiting to hear words as
fierce as from the prophet's coal -
seared lips he is visible through
a tangle of arms and bodies   as
inaccessible as behind bars
his home away from home.

His wrapped shoulder just free
of a plaster cast rests on a table
near a cane needed for an ailing
hip awaiting replacement surgery.

"Diminishments" Teilhard called
these wounds of aging
(no patience here for the embrace of
war in *The Divine Milieu*).

Diminished yet undimmed. Now
the pain and list of standing to
embrace an arriving friend do
not reach his face. Once allowed
a smile overcomes the forehead
crease, the awareness of everything
as close as the headlines: He once said:
"the preacher should preach, Scripture
in one hand, newspaper in the other."

Frown lost in smile. Again Isaiah comes to mind:
"He will speak justice to the nations without his
breath snuffing a candle, his steps bruising a blade
of grass." The unlikely blend of strength and
gentleness. *Purity of heart is to will one thing.*

Greek Revival

The opposite of Athens   here
the ruins of a neighborhood astonish
hiding and showing behind empty
row-houses an intact three-quarter replica
of a Parthenon set back on this surprise
of a lawn as precious as the silk lining
of an antique chest.

Walking or driving my long-lost schooling
draws me here by detour like the starlings
in and out the porticos nest-building or finding
perches for wherever they pass the night.

All these years I was only once inside
disappointed that some great public space
never was   from the beginning the *aula*
a subdivision into classrooms   yet

coming outside again the delight to notice
the *stoa* extending all the way around
a peristyle! Visions of Socrates striding
students in tow, robes over gesturing arms:
essences, nature, the four elements...

I notice too my arm around a great column
a balance for a glance down the porch?
No, without my knowing, an embrace
The Greek Thing! Mind ordering an
illusive world as this temple would
shape these shambles. My nostalgia for
an adventure breath-taking and beautiful
and futile finally.

Hospital Visit

Along the hall the open doors frame
wounded bodies in sheets as rumpled
as collapsed sails on shipwrecks

bringing me to the relief of this
cul-de-sac where six blind elevator
doors flank a blank wall   softened

by a large framed poster   one of those
imitations of Monet's gardens.
An imaginary opening into life away

from this place of sickness and dying.
The whole cup. All is gift. Drink the cup.
The elevator leaves me near the street

for the half-hour walk home through
streets as soiled as the sickrooms.
The sky is clear. Instead of a poster
I have an evening sky.

The Other Side of the Altar

Father or grandfather?   I can't tell
the age of his charge is blurred by
what seems like Down's Syndrome.

Side by side in a front pew
they are more a homily than
any words I am about.

A word made flesh   this old man
moving his finger across the page
of a paperback hymnal

A hint of the care that goes on at home
the long haul.
Love and patience learned by doing.

Evening Primrose

A grand country house   white
against green lawn lined
left and right with trees
holding back thick woods.

At the far end a garden
ah no, just a bean patch
gladiolas   marigolds
keeping bugs off the tomatoes.

A compost heap   a hose
running somewhere for water.
A primrose bush   lackluster
now in daylight.

Toward evening a procession
ah no, only other visitors
inviting me along to join
their vigil for sunset.

Suddenly a primrose tendril
pops. Then thirty,   no
forty flowers open one by
one   pale in summer night.

Back on the great porch I
still see them alive as
fireflies. The little moons
mirror moonlight

much as this burning bush
here at solstice as far from
December as we come is
Christmas in miniature.

Looking down on flowerflesh
unfolding I am again a child
nose in straw at a church crèche
taking in the Incarnation.

And back here a procession after all!
Not we to bush but blossom to
blossom: a Christmas procession
Shepherds and Magi

Stephen and the Innocents
John the Beloved and Becket
the Blessed leading us to Bethlehem
to light our lamps in world's night.

The Triplets

Across the room the waiting mother
has the silhouette of a ripe pear
the father is off fetching coffee for her
they are of course together in this unfolding.

Concerned about her standing
I approach with a folding chair
which she smiling waves away.

Now on Sunday mornings the five
of them fill the church as though
they were the only ones there.

Away at the altar end I am
eager for the moment I am closer
can choose which one to hold this time.

They exchange arms easily   seem to know
what a treat they are   each looking back
on his brothers as though to say:
"my turn for all this fuss".

Weekdays we are at their door
dinners clothes (matching, to be sure)
and, yes, diapers. Our extended family.

At Christmas   gift upon gift they already
are: imprinted coffee mugs   three kings in
Santa caps. Now I have them for breakfast.

Beach House

The full-length window has two panels
lower lifting into upper in warm weather.
In this season it divides my view between

endless sky   ocean   inlet   distant wetlands
and nearer: dune grass   thick tangles of briars
and the scrub pines more brown

than green in late winter. Earth colors
that keep my gaze downward   toward
another beauty than the heavens.

Even the sea birds tire of the high winds
descend and feed on the shoals of low tide.
I can be nourished here: *earth and earth's beauty.*

Strathmere, New Jersey

By late afternoon the clouds drift out over the ocean
in furrows as regular and gray as the whitecaps of
a surf surging north. Sky and sea   one canvas
drowning in the roar of a rising tide.

At this hour on a brighter evening I would move
to the far side of this house   open to the sea on
three sides for a sight of the sun falling into water.
This chiaroscuro hour keeps me here instead.

Berkeley, California

From a home snug in the hills
pine   cedar   a redwood
frame in the failing light the Golden
Gate miles off across the water

still blue under a clear sky.
Once the sun falls behind the hills
that pin the bridge to Marin County
everything changes.

Clouds gather.   As though on a pallet
mountains and sea mix their blues and greens
against the lingering light.
A hundred paintings here this hour.

And the silence. Toward the south
the Bridge joins the hills to the tumult
of the great city. From here   for now
the sea and mountains prevail. All sound
                    is hushed in the encompassing mists.

Metaphor

The theologians say their creeds are symbols
metaphors for matters we cannot comprehend
I have one here   high in the Berkeley Hills
where I wait for the sun to burn off the morning mist
so I can see the Golden Gate across the water.

One teaching I find difficult to imagine is
the soul leaving the human body.
My experience of death is an exhaustion   ending
in absence.   Perhaps the spirit departs like
the shapeless mist   disappearing as I am watching.

Photograph

Over a lifetime I notice I do not
photograph well. I look away
frown   neglect to smile   seem uneasy

Now and again I am pleased
with a picture taken unawares
my embracing a child   greeting a friend

Last week a routine appointment
a formal sitting for a clerical directory
nothing serious   twenty of us in Sunday suits

A studied pose   two or three quick flashes
I know I blinked for one of them
I expect the worst

I want to believe I am like Simone Weil
saying she could not wear any garb or uniform
that would mark her as other than ordinary

Years ago someone told me that I was
"restless in my body"
compliment or criticism I have no idea.

Particular Examen

Painful the unshielded sightings of ourselves
accidents not accidental   more poor judgment

This time I comfort myself with some words of
a friend answering a question about being a priest:
Be with and for others in ways the authorities
would call irresponsible

So for my car   lent to a young friend in hard times
towed home from a bumper car scenario   wrecking
several others   sending my man off to jail

I filter friends' comments through the Scriptures
Give to all who ask of you
Do not let your left hand know what your right is doing

I wonder too what Dorothy Day would say
no promise that such gestures work in any obvious sense

Berkeley Farmers' Market

Returning students everywhere
pizza in hand   the grass and oleander
center strip of a downtown street
the spillover lunchroom of a shop too

small for the half-inside half-outside
jazz trio serenading a queue disappearing
around the corner into plain neighborhoods
of cleaning and landscape people at the colleges

ending finally at what I want to call
a runway   without the images of snake oil
freak shows or the hustle of barkers

no, the twice-weekly transformation of
an ordinary block into a cornucopia
everything *au naturel*:   peaches   melons
plums   nectarines   with signs:
"wildly sweet" or (a nod to the organic)
"luscious, if irregular, for eating by candlelight"

these tastes   sizes   colors   never make it
back East where merchants wet and wax
the fruit to pretend a flavor lost in translation
here tomatoes recover their identity as fruit.

The young woman with a tray of samples
knows easily her slices will seduce me
without any wiles from her. All the vendors

at rough wooden counters under canopies
in front of trucks and vans reading
"Watsonville Orchards" or "Cisneros Farms"

have that leather look   that lotion-free grit
tan of the Central Valley of California
blessed by Cesar Chavez   I hope these
owners and workers hold that blessing

And music … three old black men sit
between stalls on turned-over baskets
low enough with their banjos and tambourines
to enchant the children: "Under the Boardwalk"
sung sotto voce to draw you in without overwhelm

And flowers … a woman in a granny gown
has in each hand bouquets of stunning colors
so lovely her blossoms   her uncosmetic smile
I will buy a bunch. Today is Tuesday. If Thursday
has me here again   more flowers   another smile.